Lions are the king of beasts. Thes
cats once roamed Africa, Asia and Eu
only live in central and southern Afric
National Park in India. There is only one species of lion.

D0708461

Discover 10 reasons to love them!

1 They hang out together

Unlike all other cats, lions live and hunt together in family groups called prides. All the lionesses and their young are related and they hang out with up to three different males.

In Africa, each pride patrols huge territories of sun-baked savannah.

2 They have magnificent manes

Male lions must fight each other to be the leader of the pride. They have shaggy manes that protect them from fierce bites and scratches. Two males can rule together, but sometimes just one lion will be in charge.

After two or three years, the leader of the pride will lose a fight against a rival male. Then they have to wander off alone. Over time their great manes darken with age as they battle to survive.

red-billed hornbill
older male
stargrass

3 They have a mighty roar

As day breaks or dusk falls, male lions stretch back and roar. They are warning rivals or calling out to their pride. This mighty sound can raise a cloud of dust and be heard five miles away.

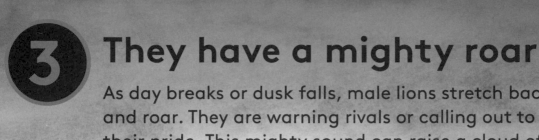

tassel
flycatcher bird
SHOW YOU LOVE A LION
Ask for a lion for your birthday! Adopt a lion through charity organisations to get fact packs and updates.

Lions also send messages with their tails. They flick them if they are cross and raise their black tassels so cubs can follow them through the long grass.

4 They think spikes are scary

Lions like eating porcupines but these prickly meals are difficult to catch. They try to flip the porcupines over with their paws. But in this dance to survive, the porcupine quills often get stuck in the lion's paws, nose or cheek.

If these barbed spikes sink deep into a lion's skin, they can lead to deadly infections. If the porcupine escapes, it simply grows more quills. So apart from humans, porcupines are a lion's worst enemy.

5 They have glow-in-the-dark eyes

A few days after they are born, lion cubs open their blue-grey eyes. Months later these turn orangey brown and shine in the dark. Lions are nocturnal and need to be able to see in dim light.

Small patches of white fur reflect low light back into a lion's eyes. This helps them see better so they can find and track their prey in the cool shadows of the night.

hyena
vulture
zebra
SHOW YOU LOVE A LION
Send Lions for Life cards! Support the Born Free Foundation and help spread the word.

6 The females are the hunters

When their cubs are hungry, lionesses slink off to hunt. They scan the landscape for the opportunity of a meal. As a team, these camouflaged cats can bring down zebras, antelope or even a giraffe.

When they spot their prey, each lioness knows exactly what to do. Some race ahead to wait in ambush while others herd the victim into their clever trap. Their success will feed the pride.

7 They have playful cubs

Lion cubs tumble over their patient, resting mothers. They chase her tail and lick her face. They fight for fun or may play with an ostrich egg that they find in the grass.

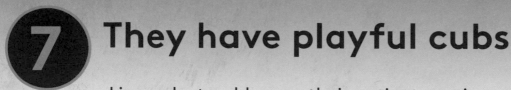

Bouncy cubs are healthy and strong. But all lion cubs are in danger if their father, the leader of the pride, loses a fight. A new male will only want his own cubs in his pride.

ostrich
ostrich egg
SHOW YOU LOVE A LION
Discover a lion's story! Watch the famous wildlife film 'Born Free' to learn about Elsa the lioness.

8 They love a catnap

Lions spend a lot of their time asleep. They cuddle up, stretch out or just flop in a pile. Some seek the shade, while others loll in the sun or hang over a branch up a tree.

If their tummies are full with a really big meal, lions slumber all day and all night...

warthog
lioness
lion

9 They rub and roll

Lions rub against each other to say hello. This greeting can be so powerful that they knock each other sideways. Their smells mingle and friendships grow.

Each lion has its own oily scent. This special smell comes from its chin, lips, cheeks, whiskers, tail and even the bit in-between its toes.

SHOW YOU LOVE A LION
Buy recycled lion poo pellets! They are said to frighten stray cats away as they think a bigger cat is on the prowl.
mugger crocodile
lions

10 They rule their land

Lions are top predators in the wild places where they live. But the survival of these big cats is threatened by trophy hunters and farms expanding into the natural habitats where lions roam.